EBENEZER BRYCE

ALSO BY HERB BRYCE

Me and the Cottonwood Tree
Beyond the Cottonwood Trees

EBENEZER BRYCE

— Bryce Canyon National Park's Namesake —

HERB BRYCE

WITH ANNA KATZ

HB BOOKS

Copyright © 2023 by Herb Bryce
All rights reserved.

No part of this book may be reproduced, or stored in a retrieval system, or transmitted in any form or by any means, electronic, mechanical, photocopying, recording, or otherwise, without express written permission of the publisher.

Published by HB Books, Shoreline, WA
www.HerbBryce.com

Edited and designed by Girl Friday Productions

www.girlfridayproductions.com

Design: Paul Barrett
Project management: Reshma Kooner
Editorial production: Katherine Richards

Front cover photograph of Ebenezer Bryce (approx. 1905), courtesy of Janet L. Alexander, Ebenezer's great-great-granddaughter.

ISBN (paperback): 978-1-7343885-7-2
ISBN (ebook): 978-1-7343885-8-9

To my dad, Howard Bryce.
He didn't say much, so when he spoke, you listened.

CONTENTS

Prologue ix

Chapter 1 Childhood and Conversion 1
Chapter 2 The Voyage Begins 5
Chapter 3 On American Soil 9
Chapter 4 Called West 13
Chapter 5 Marriage, Family, and Mills 17
Chapter 6 An Upside-Down Ship 21
Chapter 7 Mary Ann Makes History, Too 27
Chapter 8 One Family Among Many 31
Chapter 9 Homesteading the Desert 35
Chapter 10 Escaping the Cold 39
Chapter 11 Selling the Farm Yet Again 43
Chapter 12 The Bryces in Bryce 47
Chapter 13 A Pioneer Retirement 51
Chapter 14 Laid to Rest 55
Chapter 15 Bryce Canyon National Park 59

Acknowledgments 61
References 63
About the Author 65

Gloria Bryce.

PROLOGUE

"This right here is the great-great-grandson of Ebenezer Bryce. As in, Bryce Canyon. We should get in for free."

—Gloria J. (Kortus) Bryce, 1953–2017

In 2014, my wife, Gloria, and I went to visit Bryce Canyon National Park. After a couple of hours of scenic driving, we pulled up to the fee station at the visitor center, where the nice young attendant was ready for us to pay our thirty-dollar fee. In the passenger's seat, Gloria leaned forward and said, "This right here is the great-great-grandson of Ebenezer Bryce. As in, Bryce Canyon. We should get in for free."

"Nah," he said, clearly thinking she was pulling his leg.

"Go on, Herb," Gloria whispered to me. "Show him your ID."

I took my wallet out of my pocket, pulled out my license, and handed it to the attendant.

He examined it closely, looked up at me, and said, "Well, I'll be damned." Then he let us in for free.

My name is Carlos Herbert Bryce, better known as Herb Bryce. I was born in 1933, in a dusty little town in the Gila Valley of southeastern Arizona. At the time of this writing, I am eighty-eight years old, and I've continued the family tradition of writing, recording, and doing genealogical research. In fact, after sixty years living in the United States, Ebenezer Bryce traveled all the way back to his native Scotland to trace his family. He even hired a genealogist and left a thousand dollars in his will for further investigation.

Not everyone gets a national park named after them, and because of that and the Bryce family's decades of effort, I've been able to piece together my great-great-grandfather's story. Like the stories of so many people now living in the United States, it's a story of hard work, hardship, and hardheadedness.

The way we look at the past is constantly changing, and I've done my best to keep up with the times. This project and all my work is an imperfect part of that change, and I hope that it is received with lenience and a recognition of my good intentions. I have tried to provide the greater context that, historically, has been erased or disavowed and to give credit where credit is and always has been due but often withheld. I respectfully acknowledge the many people who inhabited this land and called it home before my family and other white settlers claimed it.

Ebenezer Adam Bryce.

CHAPTER 1

Childhood and Conversion

"I am going to go to America. If you stop me from going now, I will leave the day I become of legal age."

"If you will swear that you that you will be responsible for your own sins, you can go."

—Ebenezer Bryce in conversation
with his father, Andrew

In 1981, one of Ebenezer's great-great-grandsons, Mark Smith Bryce, was doing genealogy research in the Church of Jesus Christ of Latter-day Saints headquarters in Salt Lake City. There he found a brief handwritten autobiography by Ebenezer Bryce, dated November 1st/97 (November 1, 1897). According to the man himself, Ebenezer Adam Bryce was born in Dunblane in the county of Perthshire (now called Stirling) in Scotland, on November 17, 1830, to Andrew and Janet (Adamson) Bryce. They had eight children: three boys, of which Ebenezer was the youngest, and six years later, five daughters. Only two sons and two daughters survived to adulthood.

The family moved to Tullibody to be closer to the shipyards when Ebenezer was eighteen months old, and, at the age of ten, he followed in his oldest brother's footsteps and began working at the shipyard. By the time he was fifteen, he was an apprentice ship's carpenter and millwright. That skill set is what ultimately brought him across the North Atlantic Ocean to the United States.

A few years earlier, when Ebenezer was twelve years old, he had heard missionaries from the Church of Jesus Christ of Latter-day Saints—commonly known as the "Mormon Church" though the preferred nomenclature today is "LDS"—preaching in the streets. At seventeen, he again encountered a group of converts and missionaries from this religious institution that was founded by Joseph Smith in the United States, the same year as Ebenezer's birth. Seven years earlier, in 1823, Joseph Smith had claimed that he had a vision in which an angel named Moroni instructed him to excavate engraved golden plates from a hillside near his home in western New York State. His translation of these plates tells the story of an Israelite family's migration to America hundreds of years before the birth of Jesus.

A foundational tenet of the LDS faith is grounded in the Great Commission, God's commandment to "go ye therefore, and teach all nations, baptizing them in the name of the Father, and of the Son, and of the Holy Ghost: teaching them to observe all things whatsoever I have commanded you" (Matthew 28:19–20 [King James Version]; see also Mark 16:15–16). Joseph Smith emphasized the importance of missionary work from the beginning of the religion as being important to grow the Church. The Church was organized in Fayette, New York, on April 6, 1830. By the end by the year there were 289 members. Seventeen years later, in 1847, when Ebenezer was converted, there were over 34,500 members. So, we can imagine that this LDS group of sixty-three converts waiting near the Tullibody shipyard to make passage to America was excited to answer Ebenezer's questions. We don't know any specifics about that auspicious meeting, other than it propelled him toward the LDS faith.

This caused some trouble. His family were devout Covenanters in the Reformed Presbyterian Church of Scotland and held prejudiced views on the new religion. Ebenezer's father went so far as to lock up his son's clothes to prevent him from attending the meetings, though his mother had a softer heart and helped him recover his clothes so he could attend. Perhaps she regretted it when the teenager begged his father to allow him to emigrate with the group of converts—he needed his father's signature because of his status as a minor. Andrew eventually agreed, after Ebenezer raised his right hand and swore that he would be responsible for his own sins.

After Ebenezer's conversion and baptism into the LDS faith in the spring of 1848, Andrew promptly disowned him. The young man never saw his father or mother again.

Horse-drawn train. Image from Australian Railway Historical Society Collection, courtesy of University of Newcastle library's special collection.

CHAPTER 2

The Voyage Begins

"James Alan Hunter's mother [the Clackmannan parish clerk] told him about climbing the Clackmannan Tower with her father early one morning and watching the Mormons with their donkey carts stretching out for two miles or more."

—Teresa Whitehead

There is some confusion about how the John Sharp Company of sixty-three LDS converts got from Tullibody to Liverpool to make passage to the United States. Many records claim, without evidence or detail, that Ebenezer's father came aboard the ship to persuade him not to go, and that *this* was when the young man swore that he would accept all consequences. There is evidence that the group traveled from Tullibody to Glasgow by donkey cart, perhaps along the "horse-drawn railroad" that ran from Edinburgh to Glasgow. (Steam engines replaced donkey- and horsepower in the 1850s.) From Glasgow the group sailed to Liverpool in a steamboat.

There they signed up with agents of the Church who were arranging passage to the United States for 232 converts, members, and returning missionaries traveling second class from all over the UK. They proceeded through customs and boarded the HMS *Erin's Queen*, then waited two days for a good tide. On September 7, 1848, the ship set sail with 248 passengers.

One of the many histories written about Ebenezer claims that he was a stowaway for the long ocean voyage from Scotland to the United States. But would a person whom acquaintances, friends, and family members later lauded for his righteousness travel without paying? In the FamilySearch genealogy website, you can in fact find the HMS *Erin's Queen*'s passenger list with his name on it. Admittedly, it is hard to read and easy to miss.

Rather than taking the great risk of stowing away, the skilled, strong young man with ample ship-carpentry experience likely got a job on board as a way to pay for the trip. He wrote as much, claiming that he joined the thirty-fifth company of converts in the UK—called the John Sharp Company after its leader—and boarded a ship to serve in its crew, though I cannot find any historical evidence to confirm or deny such a claim.

Port of New Orleans, 1841 engraving. Photographs by A. Mondelli and William J. Bennett.

CHAPTER 3

On American Soil

"When the landlady of the boarding house in St. Louis died of cholera, I moved to Paduca, Kantuca [Paducah, Kentucky] to find work to make enough money to go to Salt Lake City."

—Ebenezer Bryce

The ship docked in New Orleans, Louisiana, on October 28, 1848, after seven weeks and two days at sea. Can you imagine what Ebenezer might have felt, having left behind the cold and damp of Scotland to find himself in a semitropical climate on the shores of the Gulf of Mexico? Whatever his feelings, he didn't report them.

The John Sharp Company kept going, boarding a river steamboat and continuing up the Mississippi River to winter in St. Louis. Ebenezer stayed behind long enough to earn the two dollars and fifty cents required for the steamboat ticket and some extra to pay for housing once he landed, then followed them seven hundred miles north to work as a carpenter and wainwright. Soon after his arrival, however, a terrible cholera epidemic broke out, killing an estimated 10 percent of St. Louis's population in the spring and summer of 1849. When the landlady of the boarding house in which he was living died from the bacterial disease, Ebenezer decided it was time to move on.

The Mormon pioneers advanced company coming over Little Mountain, July 1847. Photograph retrieved from the Library of Congress, www.loc.gov/item/95502690/.

CHAPTER 4

Called West

"Brigham Young gazed at the view and remarked, 'This is the right place; drive on.'"

—Casey Paul Griffiths, et al.

Ebenezer was one of many LDS converts to make the arduous journey west in stops and starts. For years, LDS Church members had been moving in that direction, often driven from their various settlements by persecution from non-LDS locals. They came from locations such as Fayette, New York; Kirtland and Hiram, Ohio; Far West, Missouri; and Nauvoo, Illinois. This influx of LDS members had made Nauvoo the most populated city in the state, and Joseph Smith had been its mayor, as well as the president of the Church. Smith's practice of polygamy, among other LDS practices, had incited not only people from outside the Church but many of his fellow practitioners, some of whom used the media, to air their grievances. In response, he raised a militia, which didn't win him any favors from the Illinois authorities.

He was arrested and incarcerated in nearby Carthage, where an angry mob found him and his brother Hyrum. A few years before my ancestor stepped foot on American soil, on June 27, 1844, the mob murdered the two men. Many consider this act an assassination because of its religious and political implications—Joseph Smith had just announced his bid for the United States presidency.

In 1846, Brigham Young led LDS Church members out of Nauvoo, with the goal of establishing a theodemocratic state called Deseret on a swath of land twice the size of Texas, with the Sierra Nevada mountains to the west, the Rockies to the east, the Mexican-American border to the south, and extending up into Southern California and Oregon Territory. The Salt Lake Valley was located in Mexico territory, but after the Mexican–American War and the signing of the Treaty of Guadalupe Hidalgo on February 2, 1848, the entire Southwest became US territory.

With that, Brigham Young began to call on prominent LDS leaders to lead groups of families to establish strategically located settlements throughout the proposed state of Deseret. To name a few: San Bernardino and Port San Pedro in California; the Meadows (later renamed Las Vegas) and Truckee Meadows (later renamed Reno) in Nevada; Boise, Idaho; and Snowflake (settled by Erastus Snow and William J. Flake), Mesa, and Gila Valley in Arizona; and St. George, Utah.

It was during that time that Ebenezer joined the migration. From cholera-ridden St. Louis he ventured 175 miles southeast to Paducah, Kentucky, where he earned enough money to join up with the James Pace Company, a Mormon wagon train of one hundred wagons, in March of 1850. The group departed from Kanesville (now Council Bluffs), Iowa, on June 11 and arrived in Salt Lake City, Utah, on September 16, three years behind the original LDS pioneers who settled the Salt Lake Valley.

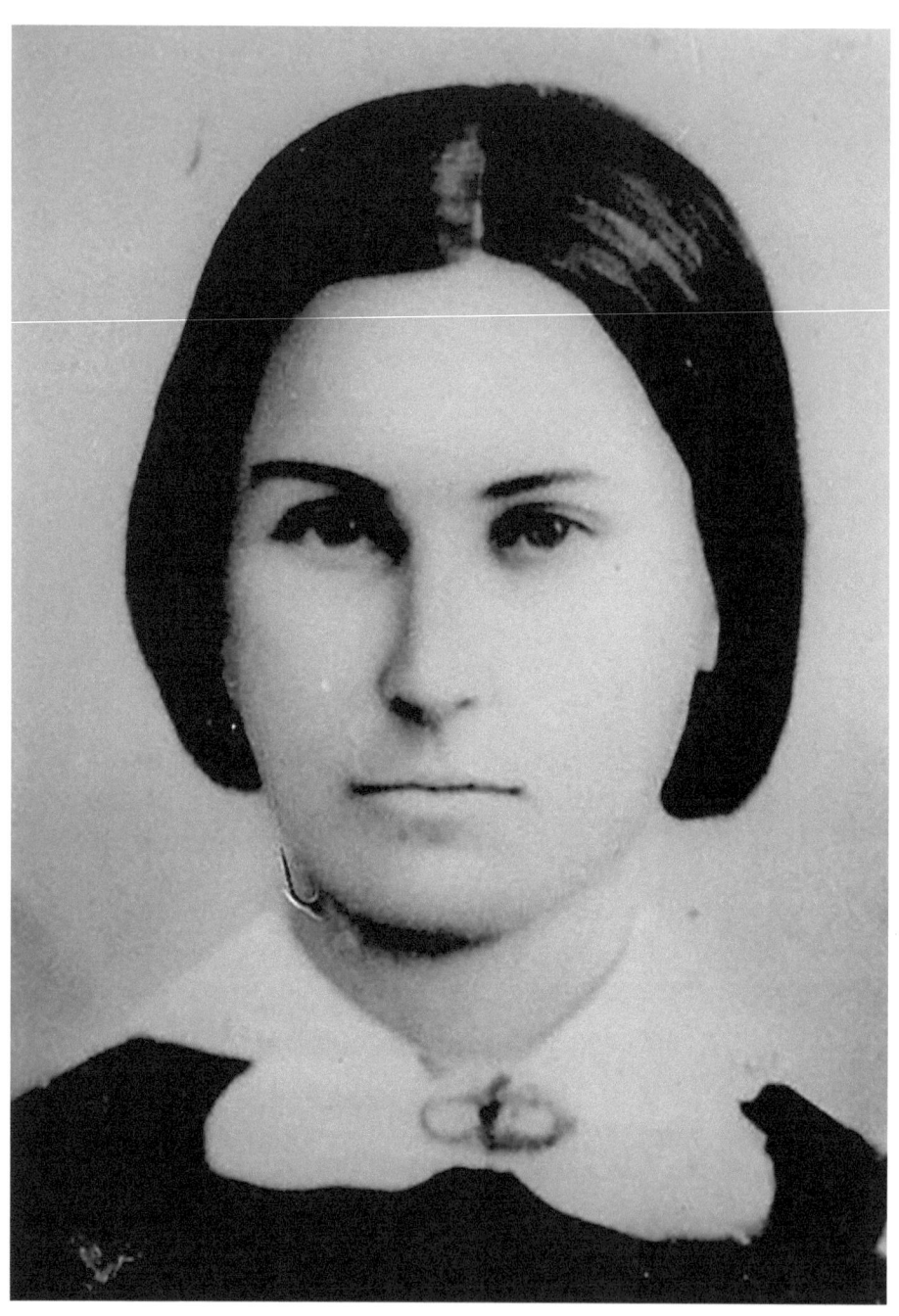

Mary Ann Park at approximately seventeen years old.

CHAPTER 5

Marriage, Family, and Mills

"Mary Ann made her own wedding dress of white crossbar with a tight-fitting bodice and full skirt."

—Janice Margaret Tiernan, FamilySearch

Ebenezer, a burly and skilled single man who would turn twenty on November 17, 1850, had no problems finding work in his new town of Salt Lake City. George A. Smith, a member of the LDS governing body Quorum of the Twelve Apostles, immediately hired him to work on his farm, where he met the maid of George's wife, Bathsheba. She was a thirteen-year-old Scottish lass by the name of Mary Ann Park, whom Ebenezer would marry three and a half years later.

Restored Benson Grist Mill. Operated 1854 to 1940s, processing wheat and corn in Tooele Valley. Photo by DE Johnson.

For the next few years, Ebenezer continued to work as work came, eventually taking a job for Archibald Gardner, the husband of Mary Ann's sister. He built and ran sawmills and gristmills along Mill Creek in Big Cottonwood Canyon in the Wasatch Mountains, fifteen miles southeast of Salt Lake City, and in West Jordan along the Jordan River.

In February of 1855, the couple welcomed their firstborn son and the author's great-grandfather, Ebenezer Park Bryce. Ann Jeanette arrived in 1857, followed by David Andrew in 1858, William Henry in 1860, and Alma Nephi in October of 1861. That same month, Ebenezer and his family got a "calling" to join George A. Smith's group to settle the area that eventually became St. George. Smith had personally requested that Ebenezer join so that he could help to build a sawmill and gristmill in Pine Valley, forty miles north of St. George, to process lumber for building and provide flour for baking in those two towns. Over the next few years, Mary Ann gave birth to three more children: twins Barbara Ellen and George Alvin in 1863, and Jane Louisa in 1867.

Pine Valley Chapel interior. Photo by Reuben Wadsworth, St. George News, *STGnews.com.*

CHAPTER 6

An Upside-Down Ship

"If a flood should come, it would float, and if a wind came strong enough to blow it over, it would never crash to pieces."

—Ebenezer Bryce

In 1867, former ship carpenter Ebenezer was asked to design and supervise the building of Pine Valley Chapel and Tithing Office. His solid reputation as a carpenter, plus his relation to LDS high official Archibald Gardner, might have had something to do with the request. He agreed, as long as he could do it his own way. Using shipbuilding techniques, he built what was essentially an overturned ship.

The thirty-two-foot by fifty-two-foot frame stands independently on a granite and limestone foundation. All lumber was ponderosa pine that had been custom milled locally in the sawmills Ebenezer himself had built. The crew constructed the walls flat on the ground and raised them into place using ropes, pulleys, and a whole lot of manpower. To make sure that they pulled the ropes in unison, Ebenezer sang a Scottish sea shanty—the end of each verse was the signal to pull. Once upright, the walls were "hung" on the basic structure and jointed in place with wooden pegs and strips of green rawhide. As the rawhide dried, it shrank and tightened the joints. No nails, screws, or bolts were used in the construction. The attic was constructed like a ship's hull, giving the chapel an oval ceiling.

On any given day, a crowd gathered to watch; kids especially got a kick out of the sea shanty and would sing it around the valley for months afterward. When the project was finished, Ebenezer was heard to say, "If a flood should come, it would float, and if a wind came strong enough to blow it over, it would never crash to pieces."

The two-story chapel served as a community meeting house, church, and school until 1919 when the school was moved elsewhere. The school occupied the ground floor, while the second, or main, floor was a multipurpose room with a stage at the east end. On Sunday, the townspeople gathered for worship; during the week, the pews could be moved to make room for potluck dinners, parties, town meetings, and dramas. The main floor was heated by a six-foot-long by four-foot-high stove, which was large enough to burn pine logs and gave off a pleasant pine fragrance. Brass kerosene lamps, four on each of the two brass chandeliers and two in each of the eight windows, created a soft glow on dark Utah nights.

The tithing office (now known as the Bishop's Storehouse) is a well-preserved sixteen-foot by twenty-seven-foot redbrick warehouse east of the chapel. Like many religious institutions, the LDS Church asked each member to tithe 10 percent of their earnings. Those living on subsistence farms did not have much

Pine Valley Chapel. Photo by Reuben Wadsworth,
St. George News, *STGnews.com.*

cash, so they paid in kind with farmed goods that were then redistributed to those in need, a tradition that lives on.

The Pine Valley Chapel, reminiscent of New England churches, stands today, at 154 years old, as the oldest LDS meeting house in continuous use. The chapel, along with the adjacent tithing office, was placed on the National Register of Historic Places in 1971.

Ebenezer and Mary Ann (Park) Bryce.

CHAPTER 7

Mary Ann Makes History, Too

"There were forty days of rain that winter while they lived in a covered wagon with five small children."

—Barb Cornia, FamilySearch

Back in the late 1860s, the powers that be were impressed with Ebenezer's work and proposed to him an even more important project: the St. George Temple. Because it was to be the first official temple, and therefore the most holy building, in the proposed LDS state of Deseret, the founders of the new temple wanted premium wood for its construction. Such lumber came from Mount Trumbull, Arizona, on the north side of the Grand Canyon. Ebenezer moved there in the fall of 1873—we can assume that he assigned his eldest son, who was by then eighteen years old, to the man-of-the-house role while he was away—and bought a steam-engine sawmill to more efficiently process the lumber. When they reached their goal a year later, he returned to Pine Valley.

During that time, Mary Ann became very ill or, as Ebenezer put it, "My wife's health [was] entirely broken and bedridden." She was advised to move to a warmer climate. This was relatively easy advice to follow given that the average annual snowfall in Pine Valley is ninety inches. That, combined with the altitude of nearly seven thousand feet, the fact that she'd given birth to eight kids, and the incredible work required to maintain a homestead, contributed to her waning health.

Histories of families in the pre–twentieth century tend to overlook the roles of girls and women. Obviously, female pioneers worked just as hard as their male counterparts, often while pregnant or nursing. (Mary Ann would go on to have four more children, Mary Isabelle in 1870, Joseph Walter in 1872, Heber Brooks in 1878, and Reuben Adam in 1880. All of her children lived to adulthood, which was quite a feat and a stroke of luck in those days.) On top of raising twelve kids, the Bryce family matriarch's responsibilities included but were not limited to planting, caring for, and harvesting the kitchen garden; canning for the winter; churning butter; making cheeses and pasta; rendering lard from pig fat; making candles and soap; sewing clothes, spinning yarn, and knitting sweaters; quilting; washing laundry by hand; and on and on and on. Without her, and without all female pioneers, survival would have been impossible.

Photo by National Park Service.

CHAPTER 8

One Family Among Many

"You can perhaps imagine my surprise at the indescribable beauty that greeted us, and it was sundown before I could be dragged from the canyon view. You may be sure that I went back the next morning to see the canyon once more . . ."

—J. W. Humphrey, U.S. Forest
Service supervisor, July 1915

In 1876, the Bryce family traded their house in Pine Valley for a flock of sheep and moved 160 miles east to a spot where a creek flows into the Paria River.

They settled in what was essentially sheer desert, at the base of the canyon between what is now Cannonville and Tropic. With an annual rainfall of eleven inches, it was not the most hospitable place to set up camp, though archeological evidence suggests that humans have inhabited the area for thousands of years. While traveling through the area, "paleo-Indians" left darts and spearpoints that can be dated back to the end of the last Ice Age. Fremont and Pueblo cultures set up agricultural communities in and nearby the canyon that lasted for thousands of years, starting around 1000 C.E. Then came the Southern Paiute people, who hunted and gathered there for a few hundred years and were called the hoodoos, or "red-painted faces." They were followed by the white men of the Domínguez–Escalante expedition of 1776, Mexican traders in the 1820s, and frontiersmen after that.

A few years before the Bryce family arrived in the area east of the Paunsaugunt Plateau, the Black Hawk War broke out between white settlers and Indigenous Americans, which led to the Navajo, Ute, and Southern Paiute nations' "resettlement." This region has a long history of similar forcible removal and relocation, often accompanied by violence against those being resettled as well as starvation and disease.

The Bryces' cabin, 1875–1881, at the base of the canyon on the east side of the Paria River.

CHAPTER 9

Homesteading the Desert

"Someday this will be a national park."

—Ebenezer Bryce, upon his first encounter
with the unique geology of the area

For the Bryces, who were newly arrived at the area, the first order of business was to dig an irrigation ditch. The livestock could live on desert grass, but the humans needed water for the garden and crops.

Even though their cabin would be placed near the Paria River, the water was below land level. Ebenezer and his four sons, aged fifteen to twenty-one, started the ditch at a higher altitude upstream so the water would flow into the fields. They also needed to clean out the river and a series of tributary springs.

Tropic Ditch. Photo by Gaelyn Olmstead, geogypsytraveler.com.

The next big job was to build a road into the canyon's amphitheater to gain access to the forest of ponderosa pines and to transport logs for firewood and for a cabin, barns, and fences. People from Cannonville three miles to the south also came to rely on the road, eventually referring to the canyon itself as "Bryce's canyon."

One day, Ebenezer wandered up into the canyon to explore. He was amazed by what he saw. While describing to his sons the shapes and colors of the hoodoos, he said, "Someday this will be a national park."

*A dirt road through the forest in the Bryce Canyon amphitheater.
Photo by Steven Jepson, thethoroughtripper.com.*

Navajo Loop Trail on the two bridges side descending from Sunset Point. Photo by National Park Service.

CHAPTER 10

Escaping the Cold

"One morning when they went to milk the cow, they found her standing dead, frozen solid."

—Family legend

In the late 1870s, the weather in what came to be called Bryce Canyon was not much better than that of Pine Valley, though there was less snow at only thirty-two inches per year. Still, it was below freezing at night more often there than in Pine Valley, and the climate did not facilitate the improvement of Mary Ann's health as the family had been hoping. In fact, after Mary Ann had her eleventh child, Heber Brooks, in 1878, she became so ill that she was confined to her bed. Shortly thereafter the family moved to Panguitch, about thirty miles northwest.

The winter of 1879–1880 had record-setting cold. As the old family story goes, one morning when they went to milk the cow, they found her standing dead, frozen solid. You can't help but wonder if that didn't influence their decision to again move farther south.

At the time, there were several Mormon settlements in what would become Arizona and western New Mexico. In the summer of 1880, three of Ebenezer and Mary's sons, David (twenty-one), Bill (nineteen), and Alma (eighteen) were sent to scout out possible new Mormon settlements in southeast Arizona and southwest New Mexico. After making a sheep-trade deal in St. Johns, Arizona, the boys split up. David traveled to New Mexico, and Bill and Alma headed south within Arizona. That fall, while her grownup children were out scouting, Mary Ann gave birth to her twelfth and last child, Reuben Adam.

The following summer David and Alma returned home, and Bill headed south across the Fort Apache Indian Reservation with three other men. Later the family got word that Bill had been killed while crossing the reservation. There is no record of their reaction upon hearing this terrible news.

Figure 2. Typical Colorado River crossing via ferryboat at Lees Ferry, circa 1890. Photo by Reuben Wadsworth, St. George News, *STGnews.com.*

CHAPTER 11

Selling the Farm Yet Again

"The main reason for its significance . . . is because it is the only place along the river for seven hundred miles with direct, easy access to the riverbank by land."

—Reuben Wadsworth, *St. George News*

In the fall of 1881, the Bryces sold the farm yet again and, instead of herding their flock of sheep over seven hundred miles, they traded most of them in Utah for sheep they would claim in St. Johns, Arizona. The sheep that they couldn't trade, they sold. They outfitted three covered wagons, rounded up their cattle and horses—over a hundred head in all—and headed for Arizona. The oldest daughter, Ann, was married, so she stayed behind in Utah. The addition of the oldest son, Ebenezer Park, or "Ebb," his wife, their twenty-two-month-old son, and their ten-month-old daughter made a group of fifteen. Ebenezer and Mary Ann's two youngest were thirty-three months and a year old, so there was a total of four children under the age of three in tow.

The group crossed the Colorado River at Lees Ferry and arrived at Silver Creek, just south of Snowflake, in November and stayed there for the winter. Much to their surprise, Bill, whom they'd presumed to be dead, rode into camp one evening. Again, there is no record of the family's reaction, though we can assume it was a joyous reunion.

In early spring the Bryces headed to St. Johns to claim their sheep. Ebenezer and David sheared the sheep and took the wool to Albuquerque, New Mexico, to sell, stopping in the salt mines on the way back to get a load of salt for the cattle.

The family continued on, camping in Williams Valley on the San Francisco River and selling their sheep in Silver City, New Mexico. On Ebenezer's fifty-second birthday on November 17, 1882, they arrived at Smithville (now Pima), a three-year-old LDS settlement in Gila Valley. They "dropped anchor" and found some land to erect a tent with a wooden floor and a stockade kitchen in front. They dug a well nearby to get clean water while searching for a location to homestead. Soon they realized that the best of Smithville had been claimed by the eleven families that already lived there and so decided to move on.

Bryce family late 1800s.
Front row: Helen, Linn (Melinda), Addie, Sarah, George, Jim, John, Nancy, Dora, May.
Back row: Ebb (Ebenezer Park), Bill, Al, Dick, Nell, Belle, Jan, Joe, Heber, Reuben.

CHAPTER 12

The Bryces in Bryce

"Ebenezer: Carpenter, millwright, shipbuilder, wheelwright [wainwright], cattleman, courageous, honest, religious, determined, independent, cultural, gardener, kind, hardworking faithful, missionary, and patriarch.

"And Mary Ann: Homemaker, seamstress, candlemaker, spiritual, devoted wife, and mother of twelve children."

—Marilyn Bryce, "The Story of Ebenezer Bryce and Mary Ann Park," *The Bryce Book: 1886–1983*

On land north of the Gila River lived a family of squatters. They agreed to move off the land in exchange for four horses. The Bryce family then applied for a post office, making it a town in 1883.

Ebenezer had earned a PhD in homesteading from the school of hard knocks and could read Mother Nature like a book.

The land next to the river was covered with mesquite thickets, which they promptly removed to make fertile land for crops and gardens.

The LDS Church authorities then asked Ebenezer and three other men to build a sawmill, planer, and a shingle mill on Mount Graham. After it was up and running, Ebenezer sold his share and returned to building the family's homestead. He and his sons cleared the land; constructed basic wood-frame houses; dug a canal for irrigation and running a flour mill; and planted wheat, corn, cane, vegetables, beans, and fruit and nut trees. They moved their livestock north of the river to graze the grassy hills and plains. This was the beginning of a vast cattle domain inherited by the grandsons of Ebenezer and Mary Ann.

Slowly other families moved in, and the homestead turned into a community named after its founder: Bryce.

Once the necessities of life had been established, it was time to build a solid house that would shelter them for the remainder of their lives. A home for Mary Ann. It was redbrick with all visible woodwork, made of the finest wood and crafted with precision and an eye to detail. It was completed in 1897.

Bryce redbrick house, back view, built 1897. It has been restored and now serves as the Ebenezer Bryce Foundation museum. Family photo, thanks to Jim Bryce.

Ebenezer Bryce at seventy-five, approx. 1905.

CHAPTER 13

A Pioneer Retirement

"Everything he did had to be perfect."

—Grandson Warner Bryce Mattice, speaking
about Ebenezer working in the garden

Mary Ann died on April 10, 1897, at the age of sixty, before the front porch of her house was complete. Eleven of her twelve children had reached adulthood. The twelfth, Reuben, was sixteen-and-a-half when she passed. She'd seen the kind of hardship that is nearly unimaginable to those alive today, and she played an essential part in her family's survival and the pioneering of the American frontier. She was buried in Bryce Cemetery in Bryce, Arizona.

After his wife's death, Ebenezer, age sixty-seven, was dreadfully ill, so much so that he made out his will and signed it on July 6, 1897. When he recovered, he "retired," a word that people who live on a farm would never have used, especially a Bryce living in the nineteenth century.

He loved to read and had a large library, and he still liked getting his hands in the soil. He kept vegetable and flower gardens, giving tender loving care to his favorite flower, the carnation. As his grandson, Warner Bryce Mattice, tells it:

> Everything he did had to be perfect. He even planted his garden by a chalk line. Many times, I helped him plant his garden. He would tie a string to a stake and have me hold the other end tight, while he would make the row with his hoe. If it wasn't straight, we did it again and again until it was perfect. Each row had to be the same width, too. He was a shipbuilder by trade so everything had to be perfect, or he would do it again and again.

He eventually traveled to Massachusetts to visit his sister Margaret Wright, who had immigrated and was the last of his living relatives. During that time, he served on a geology mission in the eastern states for one year as well as doing temple work, which meant traveling to Salt Lake City.

Headstone added to honor Bryce Canyon's namesake.
Bryce Cemetery at Bryce, Arizona.

CHAPTER 14

Laid to Rest

"While Ebenezer lies in peace, his name lives eternally."

—Herb Bryce, great-great-grandson of Ebenezer

Ebenezer was a skilled carpenter and wainwright, a specialist in industries necessary for settlements. He built sawmills that provided lumber for dwellings and flour mills that provided nourishment. He answered the call again and again, which was hard on him and his family.

He spent the last years of his life knowing that he had been true to his beliefs and gave more than he got. All in all, he had a good life. The LDS Church honored him by ordaining him a Patriarch.

*Original memorial for Mary Ann (Park) Bryce,
1897, and Ebenezer Bryce, 1913.
Bryce Cemetery at Bryce, Arizona.*

Ebenezer died of Bright's disease on September 26, 1913, at home in Bryce. He was laid to rest alongside Mary Ann, the love of his life, in the Bryce Cemetery on the edge of their property.

Thor's Hammer with Queen Victoria, dressed in white, in the background and just to the left, late afternoon. Photo by National Park Service.

CHAPTER 15

Bryce Canyon National Park

"It's a helluva place to lose a cow."

—Attributed to Ebenezer Bryce

On June 8, 1923, ten years after Ebenezer's death, the informal reference to Bryce's canyon became official when the U.S. Forest Service established the area as a national monument. Five years later, almost thirty-six thousand acres were redesignated as a national park.

Rumor has it that Ebenezer said of the canyon, "It's a helluva of a place to lose a cow." Despite members of the Bryce clan claiming that he never tolerated profanity and would never have said "helluva," the quote has become something of a motto.

The area is made up of rocky cliffs; horseshoe-shaped canyons; sprawling plateaus; forests of ponderosa pine, fir, and spruce trees; and "hoodoos." These unique geological formations are the result of the accumulation of flat rocks in the ancient

Lake Claron—the same plate tectonics that created the Colorado Plateau—and some long-term weathering and erosion, specifically "ice wedging." This last step, undertaken over the course of millions of years, transformed a wide plateau into narrower "walls," carved out "windows," and finally, whittled the rocks down into spires or "shafts."

Now, people travel from far and wide to see the creatively named hoodoos of Bryce Canyon, particularly Thor's Hammer, the Hunter, and Queen Victoria. Bryce Canyon National Park is visited by more than 2.7 million people every year.

ACKNOWLEDGMENTS

What a delightful adventure it was to work with Anna Katz again on our third book. She now knows more of who I am than just about anybody and has mastered my "voice." It's an honor to have her on my team.

Thank you to Girl Friday Productions, particularly Reshma Kooner for guiding this book through production, Paul Barrett for directing the design, and Katherine Richards for managing the editorial process.

Thank you to all the Bryces and others who have recorded the Bryce family's history over the years. It is rare to have so much information about your ancestors, and to them I am grateful and proud to be another link in the chain.

REFERENCES

Arrington, Leonard J. "Colonizing the Great Basin." *Ensign* (February 1980). https://www.churchofjesuschrist.org/study/ensign/1980/02/colonizing-the-great-basin?lang=eng.

Bryce, Fawn Smith, ed. *The Bryce Book, 1883–1983*. Self-published, Bryce, Graham County, Arizona, (no date nor ISBN). https://www.familysearch.org/search/catalog/206933?availability=Family%20History%20Library. [A collection of biographies and family histories of present and former inhabitants of the Bryce area. Available: FamilySearch.org; Family History Library, Salt Lake City, UT; Brigham Young University, Harold B. Lee Library, Provo, UT; University of Arizona Libraries, Tucson, AZ; Ebenezer Bryce Foundation, Bryce, AZ.]

Bryce, Wendell A. "Ebenezer Bryce." March 9, 1983. https://www.familysearch.org/tree/person/memories/KWJ8-YBB. [Wendell Bryce, great grandson of Ebenezer Bryce, was twelve when Ebenezer died. He was a National Park ranger and had the opportunity of serving in Bryce Canyon National Park.]

Ebenezer Bryce. "Migration, Louisiana, New Orleans Passenger Lists. 1820–1945." https://www.familysearch.org/ark:/61903/1:1:QKNP-3FD6.

FamilySearch. "Ebenezer Bryce, Memories." https://www.familysearch.org/tree/person/memories/KWJ8-YBB. [This website was a gold mine of information about Ebenezer Bryce. Not only did it have a family tree going back beyond the fifteenth century when the tail was added to the U in Bruce to give the surname Bryce, it had forty-nine documents, nineteen stories, and ninety-eight photos related to Ebenezer Bryce. Note: I read all sixty-eight documents and stories. There are some repetitions.

REFERENCES

Griffiths, Casey Paul, and Mary Jane Woodger, and Susan Easton Black. "What You Don't Know about the 100 Most Important Events in Church History." *Deseret Book*, Salt Lake City, UT. 2017.

https://www.ldsliving.com/the-myth-about-brigham-youngs-this-is-the-place-quote/s/85936.

Milton, Hunter R. "Brigham Young, The Colonizer." 2nd ed. The Deseret News Press, Salt Lake City, UT. January 1, 1941.

Ridgeway, William R. "Ebenezer's Story." (No date given.) https://www.familysearch.org/tree/person/memories/KWJ8-YBB. Also included in the "The Bryce Book, 1883–1983."

Sheffield, Sheridan R. "A tribute to those who colonized western frontier." Church News (July 20, 1990). https://www.thechurchnews.com/1990/7/21/23261595/a-tribute-to-those-who-colonized-western-frontier.

Whitehead, Teresa. "Ebenezer Bryce History." Research Report, part 1 & part 2 (October 2021). https://www.familysearch.org/tree/person/memories/KWJ8-YBB. [Teresa Whitehead's research report was by far the best, most accurate, and informative of all the sources I read.]

ABOUT THE AUTHOR

Herb Bryce is a direct descendant of Ebenezer Bryce, whose story is told in this book. Herb was born in rural Arizona in 1933 and moved extensively throughout his childhood and teenage years. After serving four years in the navy during the Korean War, he entered Arizona State University, where he received his undergraduate and graduate degrees. He pursued a career in the sciences, notably as division chair of physical sciences at Citrus College and as dean of science and mathematics at Seattle Central College. Over his forty-year career, Herb taught thousands of students, his love for teaching chemistry shining through. He was also highly active in the American Chemical Society and served on the Shoreline School Board and on the Shoreline Parks, Recreation, and Cultural Services Board for many years. He has a passion for the arts and is a cofounder of ShoreLake Arts.

In his spare time, Herb loves to travel to gain an understanding of cultures around the world. He currently lives in Shoreline, Washington, where he is an active member of his local community. His philosophy is that service is the rent we pay for living. *Ebenezer Bryce: Bryce Canyon National Park's Namesake* is Herb's third book. For more information, please visit the author at www.HerbBryce.com.

www.ingramcontent.com/pod-product-compliance
Lightning Source LLC
Chambersburg PA
CDIIW041109070526
44583CB00003B/124